Teenage Refugees From

RWANDA

Speak Out

IN THEIR OWN VOICES

Teenage Refugees From

RWANDA

Speak Out

AIMABLE TWAGILIMANA, Ph.D.

THE ROSEN PUBLISHING GROUP, INC.
NEW YORK

Published in 1997 by The Rosen Publishing Group, Inc.
29 East 21st Street, New York, NY 10010

First Edition
Copyright © 1997 by The Rosen Publishing Group, Inc.

Library of Congress Cataloging-in-Publication Data

Twagilimana, Aimable.
　　Teenage refugees from Rwanda speak out / Aimable Twagilimana. — 1st ed.
　　　　p.　　cm. — (In their own voices)
　　Includes bibliographical references and index.
　　Summary: Teenagers from Rwanda, both Hutu and Tutsi, describe the
conditions in their war-torn country that led them to seek safety and new lives
in the United States and Canada.
　　ISBN 0-8239-2443-2
　　1. Rwandan American teenagers—Juvenile literature.　　2. Refugees—
United States—Juvenile literature.　　3. Rwandans—Canada—Juvenile
literature.　　4. Teenagers—Canada—Juvenile literature.　　5. Refugees—
Canada—Juvenile literature.　　[1. Rwandan Americans.　　2. Rwandans—
Canada.　　3. Refugees.　　4. Youths' writings.]
I. Title.　　II. Series.
E184.R93T93　　1996
973'.04963—dc20　　　　　　　　　　　　　　　　　　　　　96-44219
　　　　　　　　　　　　　　　　　　　　　　　　　　　　　CIP
　　　　　　　　　　　　　　　　　　　　　　　　　　　　　AC

Manufactured in the United States of America.

Contents

Hutu refugees cross a bridge from Rwanda to Zaire in August 1994. The refugees fled civil war and ethnic violence that claimed 1 million lives.

INTRODUCTION

Rwanda is a small country in the heart of Africa. It has existed as a nation since the sixteenth century, when it was called the Kingdom of Rwanda. In the eighteenth and nineteenth centuries, Rwanda was one of the most powerful countries in central Africa.

There were three ethnic groups that inhabited the Kingdom of Rwanda: the Twa, the Hutu, and the Tutsi. The Tutsi specialized in raising farm animals. The Hutu farmed the land. The Twa hunted wild animals, picked fruit, and made pots. The Tutsi people were usually wealthy; the Hutu people were usually less wealthy; and the Twa people usually owned the least. The king was Tutsi, and most of the people who helped the king rule the Kingdom of Rwanda were Tutsi. Over time, people could move from one ethnic group to another. For example, a Hutu who owned enough cattle could become a Tutsi. A Tutsi who lost his cattle could be considered a Hutu.

At the end of the nineteenth century, European countries began to colonize Africa. Rwanda became part of the German East African protectorate. At the end of World War I, Germany lost its African colonies. The League of Nations, an international organization that preceded the United Nations, gave Belgium control of the Kingdom of Rwanda. Like the Germans, the Belgians kept the existing power structure in Rwanda. They continued to allow the Tutsi to have power over the Hutu and the Twa, even though the Hutu were the majority. The Belgians also introduced an identification system. Every Rwandan was required to have an identity card showing his or her ethnic group: Hutu, Tutsi, or Twa. As a result, it became difficult to change from one ethnic group to another.

In the 1950s, most Rwandans who were wealthy and powerful were Tutsi. At that time, under pressure from the Hutu majority, the Belgians began to place Hutu in important positions. They also began to hold elections for some positions. Since the Hutu were the majority, they were often elected. These changes were welcomed by the Hutu, but they didn't change the

Most Rwandans work in agriculture. These women work on a vegetable farm near the city of Butare.

economic status of many Hutu. The changes frightened the Tutsi.

In 1959, King Mutara Rudahigwa, a Tutsi, died suddenly. With the death of the king, the situation between the ethnic groups worsened. The tension between the Tutsi and the Hutu had been building since the Belgians changed their policies. The king was replaced by his brother, Kigeri Ndahindurwa. As the Tutsi-Hutu pressure worsened, political parties took sides based on ethnic groups. Tutsi-Hutu tension exploded on November 1, 1959, when Tutsi youths attacked a Hutu leader. When word of the attack spread, so did anti-Tutsi violence. Thousands of people, mostly Tutsi, died throughout the country. Thousands more Tutsi families, including those of the king and his close associates, fled to nearby countries. The Belgian colonial administration replaced nearly half of the local rulers, who were Tutsi, with Hutu. The result was a shift of power from the Tutsi to the Hutu.

In June 1960, elections were held in Rwanda. The main political party, the PARMEHUTU (Party for the Emancipation of the Hutu), won general elections supervised by the United Nations. In January 1961, with the support of the Belgians, PARMEHUTU got rid of the Tutsi-dominated monarchy and established the Republic of Rwanda.

Now in power, the Hutu authorities mistreated the Tutsi. They took their cattle and their land. Thousands of Tutsi left their houses and went to refugee camps or to less hostile parts of the country. Many fled to neighboring countries, including Uganda, Burundi, Zaire, and Tanzania.

Later that year, Tutsi refugees began attacking Rwanda. From 1961 to 1966, they tried to invade the country nearly a dozen times. The refugees were not successful. The Tutsi who had stayed in Rwanda were tortured by the Hutu population. In December 1963, for example, 10,000 Tutsi were killed.

After 1966, attacks by refugees stopped. But the Hutu-dominated government in Rwanda continued to discriminate against the Tutsi.

In 1973, violence against the Tutsi started again with the help of the military. They used Hutu

RPF (Rwandese Patriotic Front) soldiers travel to a base in northern Rwanda in March 1994. The RPF fighters were Tutsi refugees who had settled in Uganda.

students at the National University in Butare to spread violence in all of the country's schools. Major-General Juvenal Habyarimana, then Minister of Defense, used the anti-Tutsi violence as an excuse to take power. He staged a coup d'état, established the Second Republic, and promised national unity. He outlawed all political parties, except his own party. It was called the Revolutionary Movement for National Development (MRND). His policies maintained an uneasy peace for nearly eight years.

But one of Habyarimana's policies was "proportionate distribution" of national resources. This policy increased tensions between the Tutsi and the Hutu, and between the north (his region) and the south. The Tutsi received fewer places in high schools and at the university. They were practically excluded from the military. By the early 1980s, the number of Tutsi refugees living in neighboring countries had reached approximately 500,000.

Soon conditions in Rwanda were bad for everyone. The Hutu in most parts of the country were treated by the north-dominated government almost as badly as the Tutsi had been. Meanwhile, the economic situation worsened. Famine, government corruption, and stealing of tax and assistance money strained the existing Hutu-Tutsi and north-south tensions even more.

In October 1990, Tutsi refugees in Uganda launched a huge attack on Rwanda. They called themselves the Rwandese Patriotic Front or RPF.

Uwiba ahetse aba abwiriza uwo mu mugongo

ENGLISH TRANSLATION FROM KINYARWANDA:
When a parent steals in the presence of a child,
he is teaching the child to steal.

They were very successful in the first days of the attack. Then they began to lose ground, especially because Habyarimana received help from the French military. So the RPF began to use guerrilla warfare instead. This made them more effective.

The RPF's attack resulted in massive arrests of the Tutsi and of the Hutu political opponents inside Rwanda. The Tutsi were massacred in great numbers throughout the country, especially in the provinces favored by Habyarimana. From October 1990 until April 1994, hundreds and perhaps thousands of Tutsi were killed in all parts of the country.

On April 6, 1994, Habyarimana and President Cyprien Ntaryamira of neighboring Burundi were returning from a meeting in Tanzania. Their plane was blown up over Kigali. Some people believe the Tutsi were behind the bombing. Others believe that Habyarimana's own Hutu followers bombed the plane because Habyarimana had signed a peace accord with the RPF. Whatever the cause of the bombing, the next day, the worst period of murders in the history of Rwanda began. The people who were targeted were the Hutu who opposed the government, and the Tutsi.

The murders were carried out by the Hutu presidential guards, the army, and the infamous "Interahamwe" (literally, "those who attack together"). The Interahamwe was a paramilitary group associated with MRND, the political party of the president.

The Hutu officials who took over the government organized the murders nationwide. They used the government-run radio and press to do this. They also used the private newspapers and a private radio station, known as Radio Television des Mille Collines (RTLM). RTLM told the population to look for the "enemies" and to kill them. Those Tutsi and Hutu who could, fled to safety in neighboring countries, to Europe, or to Canada and the United States. Meanwhile, when the murders started, the RPF in Uganda invaded Rwanda again.

In July 1994, the RPF conquered the whole country and put an end to the murders. It created a government that included members of many

In 1962, Rwandan children celebrate the formation of the Republic of Rwanda. The Hutu government of the new republic treated the Tutsi poorly, planting the seeds for the violence that shook Rwanda in 1994.

parties. However, it left out the MRND and the Coalition for the Defense of the Republic. These two parties had organized and carried out the genocide that took the lives of approximately 1 million Rwandans.

The genocide left thousands of orphans, widows, widowers, homeless, and disabled. Among those who suffered most were the women and teenage girls who were abused. Many children lost the ability to speak for months after watching their parents, brothers, and sisters being killed.

The former Hutu government fled with its defeated army. They forced much of the Hutu population to go with them. Approximately 2 million Rwandans, both Hutu and Tutsi, fled to Zaire, Burundi, Tanzania, Uganda, and elsewhere. Others stayed in camps inside Rwanda.

Rwanda now has a Hutu president, Pasteur Bizimungu, and a Hutu vice president, General Paul Kagame, who is also the Minister of Defense.

After the RPF victory, thousands of refugees returned to Rwanda from Uganda, Burundi, Zaire, and other parts of the world. People who recently visited Rwanda say that new people live in the cities.

The government of Rwanda now faces two big challenges: to bring the 2 million refugees back home, and to try the more than 81,000 Hutu who are imprisoned. While many of them actually participated in the murders, observers have noted that perhaps as many as 40 percent are in prison for other reasons. Some are in prison because their property is now occupied by the military. Others are there because they have been falsely accused by their personal enemies, because they hold positions coveted by Tutsi, or simply because they are Hutu. In any case, until those responsible for the genocide are brought to justice, it will be very difficult to achieve national healing and reconciliation.

Most of the teens interviewed in this book asked that their photos not be used. They are still fearful of retaliation against family members in Rwanda.◆

Steve saw most of his family members brutally killed in Rwanda. In his new life in Michigan, he has found a welcoming community, close friends, and success in school and activities.

STEVE
I LOST MOST OF MY FAMILY

I am seventeen years old. I lived in Kigali, the capital of Rwanda, before I came to Dowagiac, Michigan, in November 1993. My sister had been living in Dowagiac for some time. She asked my parents if I could join her, and they agreed. We all knew that as a Tutsi, my chances of equal opportunity in Rwanda were very slim. A close member of the family had spent more than eight months in prison in October 1990 without any charges brought against him, simply for being a successful Tutsi. All the evils of the war launched by refugees from Uganda in October 1990 were blamed on the Tutsi group as a whole, especially the educated and the successful. We were constantly watched and harassed. Leaving the country was the best choice.

When I left, the situation was very tense in Rwanda. In October 1993, the president of neighboring Burundi, a Hutu, had been killed by members of the army. Some political parties run by Hutu extremists in Rwanda were demanding signs of solidarity with the Hutu of Burundi and revenge on the Tutsi in general. People were disappearing or being killed. The government was doing nothing to stop the violence. In 1993, there was a bombing campaign created by the government. It was designed to blame the Tutsi and the political opposition in order to justify arrests, imprisonment, and deaths. The government was clearly encouraging a policy of violence.

During the genocide in Rwanda, I lost most of my family members, including my parents, two brothers, my sister and her child, my grandmother, and my uncle. I also lost most of my friends. My only immediate family members who survived are my sister who lives here, two other sisters who are studying in Belgium, and one uncle. It was painful to watch American television and see the violence unfold. It was beyond our understanding how a human being could murder another human being with a machete, how neighbors could turn on neighbors, how children and women could participate in the killing. We cried a lot because we knew we wouldn't see our family members again. Summer 1994, that was the worst time of my life!

I was lucky to get out in time. When I arrived in the United States, my major problem was communication. Coming from a French-speaking country, my English was very poor. But everybody at school was very understanding and helpful. My teachers and my new friends showed extra-ordinary patience with me. They helped a lot during this period of transition from one culture to another and from one language to another. I also had to get used to the weather. At home, the weather is almost always nice. Most of the time it is around 68°F. But I'm used to the weather in Dowagiac now.

I very much enjoy the friendship of my classmates and their families. They have provided support since I got here. I play soccer on the school team and have received several trophies. Before I left Rwanda, I was going to Saint-André High School in Kigali. I played soccer with the school team. I was also on a first-division soccer team called Kiyovu, one of the two most popular soccer teams in the whole country. I also run track and field. I have already received offers of scholarships from colleges and universities, even though I'm only a junior. That's why I need to get very good grades in school and to continue to excel in sports.

My life here is different from the one I had in Rwanda. Here I have learned to do tasks I

Residents of the battered city of Kigali walk past the remains of a building after the civil war's end.

wouldn't have done in Rwanda. I have learned to do my own cooking, washing, ironing, and cleaning. My family could afford servants in Rwanda, so I didn't have to perform any of those tasks. Anyway, it is unusual for Rwandan males to cook, wash, iron, and clean. The Rwandan culture does not encourage that.

I may visit Rwanda in the future when I finish my studies. I don't think I can resettle there. I have lost my family. It would be like living in a foreign country.

After what happened in Rwanda, I don't have any solution for the problem between the Hutu and the Tutsi. Deep in my heart, I know that all these murders were a result of bad politics. And as the history of independent Rwanda has consistently shown, the Tutsi were the scapegoat for all the problems of the country. So many Tutsi died that it is difficult for those who survived to forgive.

I hope that people will choose reconciliation. I know it's very difficult for a Tutsi survivor, who narrowly escaped and saw his family chopped to death by a group of Hutu, not to hate all Hutu.

For my few friends who survived the killings, I wish they had a chance to study, because in the future, life will be even more difficult for those without education.◆

Jean-Paul, whose parents had died and whose sisters had fled Rwanda, found himself alone amidst the terror and violence ravaging the country. He fled to the United States, and from there moved to Canada. He plans to return to Rwanda someday.

JEAN-PAUL
WHAT IS NEEDED IS THE RULE OF LAW

live in Windsor, Ontario, Canada. I arrived here a couple of years ago after spending six months with my sister in Indiana.

I left Rwanda in 1993 because I knew I had no future there. I had just finished high school. When the civil war broke out in October 1990, my father was put in prison for being a well-known Tutsi in my native city of Butare. He died in prison with many other Tutsi. My mother had died several years before the war. When my father died, I felt completely confused. My sisters and I were at a loss; we were very close to our father. We had no other support. My brother-in-law, a university professor, was constantly harassed by the

A young RPF fighter awaits orders near Byumba, Rwanda. Many Tutsi boys came from Uganda and Zaire to join the fighting in Rwanda.

government. Wherever we went we were pointed at as the "enemy" because we were Tutsi. Later, my oldest sister, her husband, and their children fled to Italy.

Despite these traumatic events, I continued to go to school. During vacation, I had no home to go to. That's when I realized that I was an orphan in an unfriendly environment.

When I finished high school, I didn't know what to do. The war was going on. People continued to die for their ethnic group or their political ideas. Human life wasn't valued at all. One could die for anything, especially if he or she was a Tutsi or a Hutu belonging to the political opposition. Bombs were exploding everywhere—in bus stations, in hotels, in public places such as markets. Violence had become an acceptable political tool used by the Habyarimana regime. All this added to my sense of insecurity. What was even scarier was the impression that we, the Tutsi, were not Rwandans at all, or even human beings. Many Tutsi had been killed in different parts of the country, especially in Gisenyi and Ruhengeri. Many of those whom I thought were friends kept their distance. What a weird feeling to feel like a stranger in one's own country! I didn't think I belonged anymore.

I managed to join my sister who was already in the United States. After six months, I applied for political asylum in Canada.

After two years in North America, I have noticed that all societies have their own problems. But things seem to work smoothly here because there is peace. Above all, the law is respected. Nobody seems to be above the law. When I was in Rwanda, I could see that those in power seemed to follow their own laws to get whatever they wanted. They could kill people, steal public funds, and commit acts of injustice toward those they were supposed to govern. If people do not follow the law, there cannot be peace.

I enjoy living in Windsor. The only thing I don't enjoy is the cold weather, but I'm used to it now. This is a problem for anybody who leaves Rwanda. It is always like spring there.

Life is very demanding here. You have to work very hard. Welfare money will keep you alive, but you won't be able to do much with it. And you won't feel very proud of yourself. Chances for work are limited, and pay is not high. Of course, you have to find a roommate, because you cannot afford an apartment by yourself. But if you keep on trying hard, you can make a good life.

I plan to go back to Rwanda to visit the few members of my family who survived the genocide of 1994. In particular I want to visit my other sister who lives in Kigali. She is lonely now, because her two children were killed. Another sister of mine, and her daughter, were also killed. Maybe I'll resettle in Rwanda in the future, but only if there is true peace. Most of the people I knew (family members, friends, and neighbors) were killed in 1994. It would be like resettling in a strange country.

I wish and pray that there will be peace in Rwanda. For this to be possible, the whole system will have to change. Human life has to be re-spected. Nobody should be considered above the law. Nobody should use his or her position to kill another person or to take others' property. Even in North America there are racial problems, but whoever breaks the law of the land is punished according to that law.

I know that in Rwanda you can hardly persuade the Tutsi who survived the genocide to be friends with the Hutu (or vice versa). But if everybody were accountable before the law, many of the problems would be solved. The rule of law is the key to peace in Rwanda. I hope that people will understand that sooner rather than later, and that our politicians will make a better political choice founded on respect for human life and on justice for all.◆

Beatrice has finally found safety after more than a year of living in refugee camps and nearly starving. She is happy to be reunited with her father and to be living in Nashville, Tennessee.

BEATRICE
PEACE MUST REPLACE FEAR

I am fifteen years old. I live in Nashville, Tennessee, with my family. I arrived in the United States in September 1995 with my mother, my brother, and my sisters. My father came to the United States in 1992 as a student.

We lived in Kigali when the genocide began in April 1994. We felt quite helpless. My father was in the United States. He didn't know how to help us. He was very worried about our safety. Things happened very quickly. On April 6, 1994, we heard that President Habyarimana's plane had been shot down over Kigali and that he and the President of Burundi, Cyprien Ntaryamira, were dead. Everybody in the city knew something really bad was happening when the national radio

31

started broadcasting military songs. The next day, killings started in the city. We also heard that the war with the Rwandan Patriotic Front (RPF) had resumed.

When life in the city became very dangerous because of the killing and fighting, we fled from the capital. We went from place to place inside the country, from refugee camp to refugee camp, and then from country to country. After more than a year, my father succeeded in getting us refugee status in the United States. It was a miserable life, starving and waiting for my father to help us join him in the United States. We couldn't go back to Rwanda, either. What we had seen was too much to bear, and there were reports of continuing violence.

It was a great joy for us to join my father in Nashville. Life is great here. At least I know that nobody wants to kill us for our ethnicity, our place of origin, or our political views. It feels good to live in a place where you are not worried.

I go to high school here in Nashville. I'm in the ninth grade. Since I arrived, my biggest problem has been communication. Rwanda is a French-speaking country, so when I came here I couldn't speak English. I've been trying very hard to learn English. Still, I cannot catch everything my teachers and classmates say. At home we tend to speak Kinyarwanda (the language of Rwanda). But we also try to practice English. My mother tells us that she learned British English in

Rwanda. She has to get used to the American pronunciation.

School is not as difficult as it was in Rwanda. Here there are fewer courses and not so much memorization. In Rwanda, students choose their majors in high school. When I left I was in the second year of high school studying biochemistry. When I finish high school here, I want to be a biology major in college.

I miss my friends a lot. I don't even know if they survived the killings. I hope my English will improve quickly so I can make new friends here.

I wish for peace for my country so that people can do the things they love to do. Peace must replace fear. The level of violence in Rwanda in 1994 went beyond any human understanding. When a government kills its people instead of protecting them, you know there can't be hope. It may take another generation before the evil leaves Rwanda.◆

Jean-Hubert is in his last year of high school in Montreal, Canada. His mother, a human rights activist in Rwanda, was in particular danger when the fighting began. She managed to escape to Canada, and Jean-Hubert and his siblings followed.

JEAN-HUBERT
RWANDANS WANT PEACE

I arrived in Montreal in July 1994 after a long and difficult journey from Rwanda. I am nineteen years old.

When the genocide started in April 1994, I lived with my mother, my younger brother William, and my sister Sylvie in Kigali, the capital of Rwanda. My father had died long before the war. To avoid trouble we hid in our house. Through the windows we could see people being killed or running to escape. We heard many cries of pain. Soldiers and militia trained by the government carried lists of people to kill. My mother called people she knew in Kigali. They told her that killing was going on throughout the city.

Hutu refugees take shelter during a rainstorm as they return to their native village of Rubayi in 1996. They found their homes occupied by Tutsi who had been settled there by the Rwandan government.

The National Radio was being run by extremist elements of a new government. It was encouraging the population to "look for the enemy." "Enemy" meant the Tutsi, members of the political opposition, and all those who had criticized the regime of President Habyarimana.

We knew that we were in danger because my mother was a well-known human rights activist. Human rights activists and journalists were two groups of people who were massacred in the first hours of the killing. The fact that there had been a murder attempt on our mother in 1993 made us extremely nervous. We thought we would all die. We sat in the house waiting and getting as much information as we could.

Through connections in Kigali, my mother arranged to send us to our aunt in Save, near the southern city of Butare. It is the second-largest city in Rwanda. My mother could not go. She was well-known and would be recognized at the numerous roadblocks inside Kigali and between Kigali and Butare. She said she was ready to die alone, but could not bear to be killed with her children. So it was with much pain that we left her alone in the house and ventured through the city. With our identity cards that showed that we were Hutu, we passed the roadblocks without a problem. Roadblocks, as everybody knew, were established not really to check people's identities but to check which ethnic groups they belonged to. All those whose cards showed that they were Tutsi were killed on the spot, beaten, or stabbed with machetes. We saw many dead bodies at the various roadblocks.

The region surrounding Butare resisted the call to kill and remained relatively calm for two weeks. When killing started there, we hid in our aunt's house. We were saved because she had a watchman. But the threat to kill us increased when my aunt hid a Tutsi. People said that he used to brag about a Tutsi victory. My aunt had hidden him in the ceiling. It was a very tiny and dark space, but he had no choice.

The killers somehow got word that he was at my aunt's house. They eventually forced the door open and killed him. We thought we would be killed, too. We had hidden a person they called an enemy, thus we were friends of the enemy. We were saved at the last minute by a soldier who had been a friend of my father in the army. Otherwise our tears and pleas would not have saved us. I will never forget the cruelty with which the Tutsi was killed, despite his pleas for mercy. We felt helpless because there was nothing we could do to save him.

Shortly after our departure from Kigali, my mother moved to Canada. In the past, she had suffered because of her human rights activities. In fact, a squad had once crushed a car in which she was driving. Afterward she received threatening notes saying that she wouldn't escape alive the next time. She still bears the scars of that attack.

When the 1994 killings started, she thought she would not escape. We were all afraid for her, but also for ourselves.

It was almost impossible to get out of Kigali. Our mother couldn't find anybody to pick us up from Butare, which is very far from Kigali. It was a hard choice she had to make: stay and probably be killed, or leave us in the relative safety of Butare and save her own life. She made a wise choice because her life was in more danger than ours.

From Canada, she arranged for us to join her with the help of Rwandan and Burundian friends. First we were taken to Burundi, where we stayed for a short time. From there we flew to Kenya and then to France.

Since we did not have Canadian immigration papers, the police at the airport in Paris did not allow us to board the plane. William, Sylvie, and I were quite upset. This was our first time ever out of Rwanda, and we did not know about immigration requirements. We assumed that because our mother was already in Canada, we would also be able to go there. Eventually, the airport authorities received a message from the Canadian ministry of foreign affairs allowing us to enter Canada. We later found out that our mother had obtained help from people in Ottawa.

I will never forget the many neighbors killed, the numerous corpses on the roadblocks, the Tutsi killed at my aunt's house, and the innocent children murdered without even knowing why. I felt sad at being unable to do anything. I knew that it was terribly wrong for innocent people to be killed.

I'm very happy here. I go to high school. I'm a senior now. People are very nice here. I have made many friends. When I arrived, I was impressed by the high buildings and by the different mentality. The only thing I don't like here is winter. It's very cold.

Life is difficult here in some ways. You are on your own. You do your own cooking, washing, and ironing. In Rwanda, my mother could afford to use servants, so I had never done housework before. When we arrived, my mother decided to let my sister and me be on our own. So I share an apartment with a friend, and my sister lives with a roommate. By living on our own, we will learn the Canadian way.

Some of my friends who survived the genocide and still live in Rwanda tell me that they have no teachers. They can't study well. Because of that I don't think I will go back to Rwanda now. Here I can get a good education. If things change and enough good teachers are found, maybe I will consider going back to Rwanda. I plan to do medical or computer science studies in Canada when I finish high school.

What I wish for my fellow Rwandans is peace. I believe that with good politicians, it is possible to have peace in Rwanda. When the final analysis of this terrible event is made, I am sure people will learn that it was the fault of politicians. They thought that they could sacrifice innocent citizens who had nothing to do with politics. Instead, the genocide has created enormous problems that will take years and years to resolve. For peace to be a reality, there must be justice for all. All those who participated in the genocide must be brought to justice.

I'm a Hutu, but I have never felt anything against the Tutsi. To be honest, it is difficult to distinguish a Hutu from a Tutsi. Many times I have heard that Tutsi were taller than Hutu and had lighter skin. But this is not always true because there are tall Hutu with light skin and short Tutsi with dark skin. In fact, without identity cards, it would have been almost impossible to guess who was who. Thus the identity card was the symbol of both life and death. The one that read "Hutu" meant life, the one that read "Tutsi" meant death.

When I was in high school in Rwanda, Hutu students used to beat and threaten Tutsi students, especially during the night. But I always remained friends with the Tutsi. I always tried to protect them, and as a result I myself was threatened. Even here in Montreal, our soccer team includes both Hutu and Tutsi teenagers. I continue to believe that violence occurred and continues to occur because of bad politicians. As far as I know, the majority of Rwandans love and want peace.◆

William Jean-Robert is Jean-Hubert's younger brother. In his fifteen years he has seen many terrible things. Although it has taken some time, he has adjusted to his new life in Canada.

WILLIAM JEAN-ROBERT
I'LL NEVER FORGET

I am fifteen years old. I came to Montreal in July 1994 with my sister Sylvie-Clementine and my brother Jean-Hubert. Our journey from Rwanda to Canada was long and difficult.

I'll never forget the fear that overtook the whole city of Kigali in April 1994, when we learned that the plane that was taking Presidents Habyarimana of Rwanda and Ntaryamira of Burundi from a meeting in Tanzania to Kigali airport was shot down. I could see that my mother was worried. When I couldn't go outside to play for a whole day, I knew that the situation was really bad. When I saw soldiers and militia roaming the city, I understood that the situation was terrible. As hours passed, I got the impression from my mother's face that we wouldn't live for long. My mother had been targeted before. In my mind, I thought this would be her end.

One day we heard our mother pleading with someone over the telephone asking with desperation in her voice that her children be evacuated to Butare, where there were no killings yet.

At the roadblocks we passed, we were saved by having Hutu identity cards. It had never occurred to me that human beings could be so cruel to other human beings. As we passed through the city we could see dead bodies. At the roadblocks, we saw many more. I don't think that I have seen even an animal killed the way human beings were killed, simply because they were Tutsi or because they were opposed to the government's policies.

I was very happy to arrive in Canada, far from that unspeakable violence. I go to high school now. I'm in the third year. I enjoy being here. When I arrived I had some problems with com- munication. I speak French, but it took me some time to get used to the Québec French.

Life is agreeable, even though I work more than I used to. There is more entertainment here. People have more fun here than in Rwanda. Of course, life was great in Rwanda before the war. War destroyed everything: people, houses, nature, fun, and even hope. Young children were killed. Many people were forced to kill. Many others saw their families killed. Many bear scars from the violence. Rwanda lost its innocence and hope. I'm lucky to be out of Rwanda. What is the use of growing up in a country controlled by fear?

I called my friends who stayed in Rwanda. They told me that life is very difficult there. I wish they had the chance to come here, too.

Here I have learned to do things I hadn't done in Rwanda like cooking, washing, and cleaning. But I also have time to do things I love: playing soccer and having fun with friends. I miss our house in Rwanda, our neighborhood, and my friends. Fortunately, I have made many new friends here, and I'm now used to the cold weather of Canada.

When I finish high school, I'd like to go to college. I want to be a lawyer or a comedian. I'll see when the time comes.

If there was peace in Rwanda, things would improve. But peace is difficult after the genocide. I cannot look in the eyes of someone who has killed my relatives and friends and tell him or her, "I pardon you." It is very difficult. But I hope that this will happen sooner rather than later, because hate and violence do not solve problems. They only lead to more hate and violence.◆

Sylvie-Clementine is the older sister of Jean-Hubert and William. Like them, she has had to adjust not only to living in a new country, but also to living independently. She had a very frightening experience in Rwanda that still terrifies her today.

SYLVIE-CLEMENTINE
I WAS SCHEDULED TO BE KILLED

'm twenty-one years old. I've been living in Montreal since July 7, 1994. My brothers William and Jean-Hubert and I joined our mother, who had arrived three months earlier. I'm in my last year of high school. If I'm lucky enough to receive a scholarship, I plan to go to college next year, I hope in Québec.

Although I enjoy living here in peace and security, my life is harder here than it was before the war in Rwanda. There my mother could afford servants, so we did not have to cook and wash and work. All I had to worry about was my schoolwork. After school here, I do my homework, but I also have to cook my food and do my washing and cleaning.

Rwandan refugees line up for food at a refugee camp in Tanzania. It is estimated that the civil war made refugees of 2 million Rwandans.

When we arrived, our mother wanted us to learn the Canadian way, so we had to find our own apartments and roommates. We are on our own. Although it was difficult in the beginning, I'm now used to it. I feel more responsible. I have had two jobs so far. I was a babysitter for a while, and now I'm a cashier in a store.

The reason I want to attend college in Québec is simple. When I first arrived here, I felt very lonely. I left my friends (both Tutsi and Hutu) in Rwanda, and a number of them were killed. Now I have made many new friends here in Montreal. I don't want to leave them. I understand it's good to make friends in different parts of the world, but

I feel that I need to spend more time with the friends I have made here.

Of course, I miss my friends in Rwanda. There were some who died and others who were lucky to survive the genocide. I also miss the good times I used to have on the beach of Lake Kivu during my vacations. Despite what happened there, Rwanda is a beautiful country. I enjoyed visiting its different regions. My bad memories about Rwanda are due to the massive killings.

On a more personal level, shortly before the April 1994 crisis, I was traumatized one night when I learned that a group of girls, myself included, were to be killed. I attended an all-girl boarding school. The other girls were Tutsi. I was scheduled to be killed because my mother had consistently reported the violence of the government. She was working with national and international human rights organizations to prevent violence in Rwanda.

It was a friend who told me of my terrible danger. I didn't know what to do. If I tried to report the plot, the school authorities would call me a troublemaker, and I surely would be expelled. On the other hand, I knew that similar killings had taken place in other schools, especially in the provinces of Gisenyi and Ruhengeri, where a number of Tutsi and students from the south had been killed in the previous year. During the night, I nearly suffered a heart attack because of fear. I felt pain in my heart. I

Refugee orphans who lost their parents in the violence wait to be transferred to a camp in Zaire.

didn't close my eyes once. For some reason, the news of the killings had spread, and the whole thing was called off. But I kept asking myself why people would want to kill others. We had done nothing wrong. We were just young people trying to learn. I couldn't understand, and that's what shocked me most: the inability to find an explanation for what could have happened to me and the other Tutsi girls. Sometimes I'm still scared. Sometimes I still feel pain in my heart.

When violence began in Kigali on April 6, 1994, I was on vacation from school with my two brothers and my mother in our home in Kigali. Seeing and hearing about these killings reminded me of that terrible night at school. I thought there was no way out this time. They would surely come after my mother again. I began thinking about what we would do without our mother, forgetting for a moment that if the killers came, they would kill us, too. When she told us that we had to go to Butare without her, I thought I wouldn't see her again. But we had no choice.

Even though I don't like the weather, I enjoy living here. I enjoy shopping very much. I like the many choices that are offered in stores.

I would like to go back to Rwanda but only after I finish my studies, and only if there is peace. I know some of my friends were killed and some survived. I wish the survivors could come here and enjoy at least peace in their minds. They saw many terrible things in 1994. They cannot feel secure in their minds when they still see traces of the violence every day.◆

Didier and his family made a hasty escape from Rwanda because his father's life was in danger. He now lives in Ohio.

DIDIER
WE WERE LUCKY

I am a Hutu. I used to live in Kigali. I'm thirteen years old. I now live in Oxford, Ohio. I arrived in the United States shortly after the killings started in Rwanda. I came with my family.

I had lived in the United States when I was a small child, and my father was a student at a university. That's how I learned to speak English. When we came back last year, I didn't have any problem communicating in English.

I like living here. I'm in the eighth grade. After school, I take karate classes, go to the library, and do my homework. My dad helps me a lot. He wants me to be successful. I enjoy everything here—I'm not difficult to please.

A United Nations soldier stands guard in Kigali in May 1994. The UN attempted to keep peace in Rwanda as violence spread across the country.

I didn't experience much of the violence in Rwanda. We left only three days after the beginning of the killings. We had to get out very quickly, because my father was targeted. He was a prominent member of the political opposition and director of the National Radio. He had strongly resisted the use of radio for stirring up hate. The previous directors, members of Habyarimana's political party (MRND), had used the radio for this.

When the President's plane was shot down over Kigali, the military put in place an extremist government, and my father, who was already in hiding, was immediately replaced by an extremist director. The radio began a hate campaign telling people to look for the enemy (meaning the Tutsi and the political opposition). My father knew that he was on the list of those who had to die—his immediate boss, the minister of information, a Hutu, was among the first opposition leaders who were murdered by the Presidential Guard. We all knew that if they came for my father, we would all die. Fortunately, he managed to secure places on planes that were taking people away. We had to pack some basic necessities very quickly and go. From Kigali, we went to Nairobi, Kenya. My father applied for political asylum in the United States. We were very lucky to be able to come here.◆

Clement's friends and neighbors have made it easier for him to adjust to life in his new home. An accomplished athlete, he has had to learn to live on his own and try to cope with his terrible memories.

CLEMENT
NEIGHBORS KILLING NEIGHBORS

I came to Dowagiac, Michigan, in April 1992. I used to live in Kigali. I'm seventeen years old. I came with the help of my brother, who had been here for more than three years. He had left Rwanda because he had been refused admission to graduate school because he is a Tutsi. Rwanda had a system of regional and ethnic quotas in public high schools and in the national university. Many Tutsi were left out in the name of "regional and ethnic balance" at all levels of national life.

Like my brother, I left Rwanda because I believed I had no future there. The civil war that broke out in October 1990 had victimized the whole Tutsi ethnic group. In many areas, especially in the northern and northwestern parts of the country, hundreds of thousands of Tutsi were massacred with the encouragement of the government. There was no hope for the Tutsi as long as the war lasted. I was very depressed growing up in this environment, especially when members of my family were harassed and imprisoned without any charges. The Tutsi were often referred to as the enemy. Some members of the government were calling for the murder of all Tutsi.

When I left Rwanda, I was in the seventh grade. When I arrived here, I had serious problems because I didn't speak English. My teachers and my classmates and their parents were very patient and helpful. I was lucky to meet very nice people in Dowagiac. I'm very grateful to them. They helped me with my English and invited me to parties on weekends. This helped me to have fun and learn English. I now feel that I belong in this community.

In addition to learning English, I also had to learn cooking, washing, cleaning, and similar tasks because in Rwanda boys usually don't perform those jobs. Back home we always had a servant to do them. Here I had to learn to be on my own in many ways.

I'm a high school senior. I have made many friends. I play different sports: football, basketball, and soccer. I am very good at soccer. I'm on the school soccer team. I plan to go to college next year. I hope to get a scholarship.

When the tragic events took place in Rwanda in April 1994, I could not believe what I saw on television. Although we had seen signs of violence, we could not understand how human beings could commit such atrocities. It was very painful to see or hear news of family members and friends who had been killed. It was a very bad feeling to see neighbors killing neighbors in the most violent manner. I will never forget those evenings when we would watch the news and then sink into a terrible silence, unable to speak because of the overwhelming nature of what we had seen on the news. Again we were lucky to have caring and thoughtful friends in Dowagiac. I don't know how we could have coped without their moral support.

I'll go back to Rwanda in the future to visit and maybe resettle and help rebuild the country. But I'll go only if there is real peace. After what happened in 1994, it is difficult to imagine real peace in the near future. It is not easy to erase the memory of nearly 1 million people killed between April and July 1994. What I wish for Rwandans is that they give peace and reconciliation a chance. We cannot continue on this dangerous cycle of violence. Where is our humanity?◆

Glossary

atrocity A brutal, cruel act.

boycott Campaign to refuse to deal with a person, store, or organization to express disapproval of conditions.

colonization When a foreign nation establishes a colony against the will of the overthrown country.

coup d'état The violent overthrow of a government by a small group.

ethnic Relating to a large group of people of similar racial, national, or religious background.

extremist One who has very strong, radical political beliefs.

genocide The intentional destruction of a racial, political, or ethnic group.

human rights activist Person concerned with the conditions of groups living under repressive political conditions.

massacre The killing of a number of helpless persons.

paramilitary Term used to describe a force that is formed using the military as a model.

policies Courses of action mandated by a ruling body.

"proportionate distribution" A system where natural resources are divided among groups of people according to the size of the group.

protectorate A relationship between two countries where one has authority and the other is dependent.

reconciliation Restoration of friendship after a period of conflict.

refugee Person fleeing his or her home to escape persecution.

For Further Reading

Eegley, Randall. *Rwanda*. New York: ABC-CLIO,
    1993.
Isaac, John. *Rwanda: Fierce Clashes in Central
    Africa*, 1st ed. Woodbridge, CT: Blackbirch
    Press, 1996.
Oliver, Roland, and Fage, J. D. *A Short History of
    Africa*. New York: Facts on File, 1988.

Challenging Reading

Prunier, Gerard. *Rwanda Crisis: History of a
    Genocide*. New York: Columbia University
    Press, 1995.
Watson, Catherine. *Exile from Rwanda:
    Background of an Invasion*. Washington, DC:
    U.S. Committee for Refugees, 1991.

Index

ABOUT THE AUTHOR

Aimable Twagilimana, Ph.D. was born in Butare, Rwanda. He holds bachelor's and master's degrees in English from the National University of Rwanda, a master's degree in Applied Linguistics from the University of Reading in England, and a Ph.D. in American Literature from the State University of New York at Buffalo. He is currently a professor of English at Buffalo State College. He recently published a novel, *Manifold Annihilation*.

PHOTO CREDITS

Cover, © Paula Bronstein/Impact Visuals; pp. 6, 15, 18, 22, 24, 30, 36, 42, 46 © AP/Wide World; pp. 9, 52 © Sean Sprague/Impact Visuals; pp. 13, 26, 34 © Crispin Hughes/Impact Visuals; pp. 48, 54 © Teun Voeten/Impact Visuals; p. 50 © Hien Lam/Anako; p. 56 © Archive Photos/Express Newspapers.

LAYOUT AND DESIGN

Kim Sonsky